Pennie Stoyles

The A–Z of
Health

Volume 4 K–O

Smart Apple Media
P.O. Box 3263
Mankato, MN, 56002

First published in 2010 by
MACMILLAN EDUCATION AUSTRALIA PTY LTD
15–19 Claremont St, South Yarra, Australia 3141

Visit our web site at www.macmillan.com.au or go directly to www.macmillanlibrary.com.au

Associated companies and representatives throughout the world.

Copyright © Pennie Stoyles 2010

Library of Congress Cataloging-in-Publication Data

Stoyles, Pennie.
    The A-Z of health / Pennie Stoyles.
        p. cm.
    Includes index.
    ISBN 978-1-59920-541-0 (library binding)
    ISBN 978-1-59920-542-7 (library binding)
    ISBN 978-1-59920-543-4 (library binding)
    ISBN 978-1-59920-544-1 (library binding)
    ISBN 978-1-59920-545-8 (library binding)
    ISBN 978-1-59920-546-5 (library binding)
    1. Medicine, Popular--Encyclopedias, Juvenile. 2. Health--Encyclopedias, Juvenile. I. Title.
    RC81.A2S76 2011
616.003--dc22

                                                        2009038467

Edited by Julia Carlomagno and Gill Owens
Text and cover design by Ivan Finnegan, iF Design
Page layout by Raul Diche
Photo research by Legend Images
Illustrations by Andy Craig and Nives Porcellato, except for pp. 4 (top), 8, 9, 20 (Guy Holt) and pp. 6, 22, 26 (Jeff Lang)

Manufactured in China by Macmillan Production (Asia) Ltd.
Kwun Tong, Kowloon, Hong Kong
Supplier Code: CP December 2009

Acknowledgments
The author and the publisher are grateful to the following for permission to reproduce copyright material:

Front cover photo of medicines © Mihnea Simian/Shutterstock

Photographs courtesy of:
Artville/burke triolo productions, **18** (milk); Bananastock, **30**; © Steve Hix/Somos Images/Corbis, **15**; Corbis RF, **18** (spinach); Digital Vision, **18** (banana); © Markwaters/Dreamstime.com, **11** (bottom); Manchan/Getty Images, **17**; imagelibrary, **18** (tomatoes); © 2008 Jupiterimages Corporation, **14**, **23** (left), **24**, **29**; NASA/HSF, **25**; National Library of Medicine, Images from the History of Medicine (IHM), **19** (bottom), **20** (bottom); Newspix/News Ltd/Keryn Seidel, **16**; Photodisc, **30**; Photolibrary/Rüdiger Dichtel, **21**; Photolibrary/Lowell Georgia, **12**; Photolibrary/Eddie Lawrence/SPL, **7**; Photolibrary/Life In View/SPL, **5**; Photolibrary/Alfred Pasieka/SPL, **13**; Picture Media/REUTERS/David Gray, **27**; © Radu Razvan/Shutterstock, **23** (right); USAID/Solene Edouard-Binkl, **11** (top); Wikimedia Commons by Kauczuk, **19** (top).
Map based on data from Center for Disease Control, **10**.

While every care has been taken to trace and acknowledge copyright, the publisher tenders their apologies for any accidental infringement where copyright has proved untraceable. Where the attempt has been unsuccessful, the publisher welcomes information that would redress the situation.

Health

Welcome to the exciting world of health.

The A–Z of Health is about the healthy functioning of the body and mind.
Health can mean:

- physical and mental health, including different body processes
- diseases and illnesses that affect health and well-being
- drugs, treatments, and ways to stay healthy

Volume 4 K–O   Health

They Said It!

"The person who has health has hope; and the person who has hope has everything."
Arabic proverb

The kidneys are organs that clean wastes out of the blood and produce urine.

How Kidneys Work

Kidneys are complex organs that perform several functions. They regulate the composition of the blood, control the amount of water in the body, remove wastes, and help control blood pressure.

Kidneys filter the blood to provide **nutrients** to the body. Blood flows into the kidneys and **blood plasma** is filtered into thousands of tiny tubes called nephrons. Nutrients that the body needs are sent back into the bloodstream, while wastes are sent to the bladder as urine.

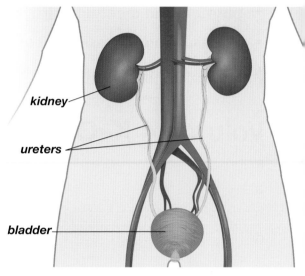

kidney

ureters

bladder

The kidneys are connected to the bladder by tubes called ureters.

Urine

Urine can range in color from pale yellow to dark brown, depending on how much water a person has been drinking. Pale urine means that a person is drinking enough water. Dark urine means that the kidneys have absorbed water out of the urine and back into the bloodstream. People with dark urine need to drink more water.

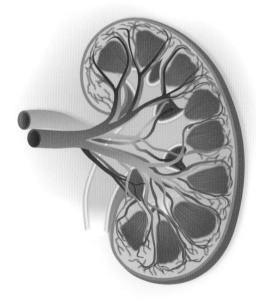

The kidneys contain thousands of nephrons, which filter blood plasma.

Did You Know?

Urine can change color according to the foods a person eats. If a person eats a lot of beets, his or her urine may turn a pinkish color.

Healthy Kidneys

Kidneys are important organs, so people should look after them. Overweight or unfit people often have high blood pressure, which can damage the kidneys. People should eat a balanced diet, drink lots of water, and exercise to keep their kidneys healthy. Infections and **diabetes** (say duy-UH-beet-EEZ) can also damage the kidneys.

Kidney Disease

Kidney disease is common in **developed countries**, and there is no cure. Some people with kidney disease have to use a dialysis (say duy-AH-luh-SUHS) machine every few days, which filters their blood. They also have to control the amount of food and drink they consume. Some people have operations called kidney transplants to replace their damaged kidneys.

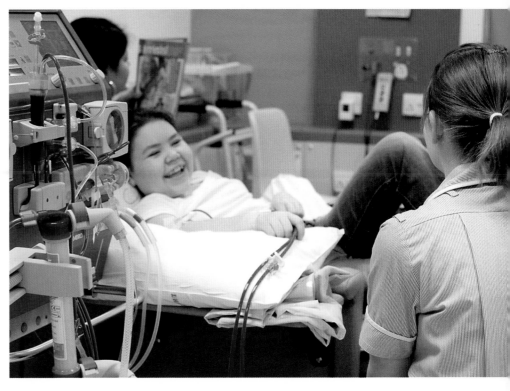

People with kidney disease sometimes use machines called dialysis machines to do the work of their kidneys.

HEALTH PROFESSIONALS: Urologists

Urologists are surgeons trained to operate on kidneys and other parts of the urinary system, including the bladder and the connecting tubes.

GLOSSARY WORDS

nutrients	food or chemicals that the body needs to survive
blood plasma	the liquid part of the blood, without the blood cells
diabetes	a disease in which a person has too much sugar in the blood
developed countries	countries with strong economies and industries

Liver

The liver is a large organ in the body, located below the ribs. It is an important part of the **digestive system**.

How the Liver Works

The liver works as a processing factory for the body. It performs many functions.

- The blood carries nutrients and other chemicals to the liver. The liver breaks down and changes the **nutrients** to make them easier for the body to use.

- It breaks down poisons so they can be removed from the body.

- It makes a substance called bile, which helps the body digest fats.

- It removes iron from dead red blood cells so it can be recycled and used to make new ones.

liver

The liver is located beneath the ribs and performs many important functions.

Did You Know?

In ancient times, people used to believe that feelings were controlled by body fluids. They thought that if the liver produced too much bile, it was a sign of anger.

Liver Damage

A healthy diet can help keep a liver healthy. If a person is overweight, fat can build up around the liver, preventing it from working properly. Alcohol is processed in the liver, but too much alcohol can kill liver cells and even leave scars. This is called cirrhosis (say si-RO-suhs). Poisons and infections, such as hepatitis, can also cause cirrhosis.

Jaundice

Jaundice occurs when the skin and the whites of the eyes turn yellow. Jaundice is often a sign of liver disease. When red blood cells die, **bilirubin** (say bil-ER-roo-BUHN) forms in the blood. Normally, the liver breaks down bilirubin, but if there is too much the liver cannot handle it and the bilirubin makes the skin turn yellow.

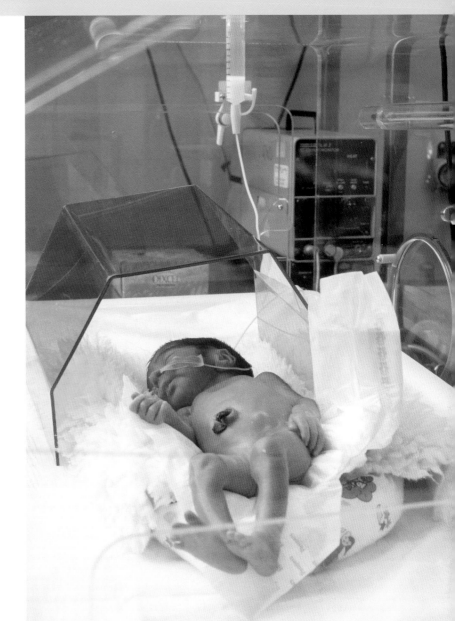

This baby has jaundice, which is caused by large amounts of bilirubin in the blood.

Did You Know?

The liver is the only organ that can grow back. A person can have up to three-quarters of his or her liver removed and it will grow back.

GLOSSARY WORDS

digestive system	a system of organs and glands that processes food and turns it into energy
nutrients	food or chemicals that the body needs to survive
bilirubin	a reddish-yellow substance that causes the skin discoloration seen in jaundice

Lungs

The lungs are organs that form part of the **respiratory system**. When a person breathes, air goes in and out of the lungs.

How Lungs Work

The lungs pass air into the bloodstream. When a person breathes in, air travels down the windpipe, or trachea, and into the lungs. The lungs are full of tiny air sacs called alveoli (say al-VEE-oh-LI), which are surrounded by **blood vessels**. When air gets into the alveoli, it passes into the blood vessels. The oxygen in the air is absorbed by the red blood cells, while the carbon dioxide moves into the lungs so it can be breathed out.

Lung Capacity

Healthy lungs have a large lung capacity, which allows people to absorb large amounts of oxygen from each breath of air. Exercise can strengthen breathing muscles around the lungs and increase lung capacity, while unhealthy lifestyles or lung illnesses can reduce lung capacity. Doctors sometimes measure lung capacity to check the health of the lungs.

alveoli

FIRST AID
Mouth-to-mouth Resuscitation

Mouth-to-mouth resuscitation is used to force air into the lungs when someone is not breathing properly or has stopped breathing. People can be trained in how to perform mouth-to-mouth resuscitation properly so they are prepared in case of an emergency.

Air travels through the lungs into the alveoli, and then passes into blood vessels so oxygen can be absorbed into the blood.

Lung Infections and Diseases

People can sometimes develop lung infections or diseases. Pneumonia is a lung infection in which the lungs fill with liquid. It can usually be treated with **antibiotics** (say an-TIE-buy-OT-iks). Tuberculosis (TB) is a lung disease caused by bacteria. It once caused many deaths, but today there is a **vaccine** that can prevent it.

Emphysema and Lung Cancer

People who smoke cigarettes may develop emphysema (say em-FUH-see-MAH) or lung cancer. The chemicals in cigarettes destroy the lungs' alveoli. Emphysema is a disease in which the alveoli become less flexible and keep collapsing, making it difficult for them to fill up with air. Lung cancer is a disease in which the alveoli are completely destroyed.

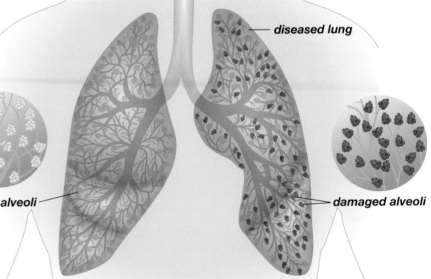

diseased lung

healthy alveoli

damaged alveoli

Lung cancer destroys the alveoli until the lung becomes shriveled and blackened.

Did You Know?

The lungs cannot move. When a person breathes, the muscles between the ribs and the diaphragm move to make the lungs move.

GLOSSARY WORDS

respiratory system	a system of organs and tubes that controls the body's breathing
blood vessels	tubes, such as veins or arteries, which blood travels through
antibiotics	substances that can kill microscopic cells called bacteria
vaccine	a small dose of a virus or bacteria injected into patients to help their bodies fight off disease

Malaria

Malaria (say mah-LAIR-ee-AH) is a deadly disease that is carried by mosquitoes in tropical areas of the world.

How Malaria Works

Malaria is caused by tiny organisms called plasmodia (say plaz-MOH-dee-AH), which are carried by mosquitoes. When a mosquito carrying plasmodia bites a person, it draws blood and allows the plasmodia to enter the bloodstream. The plasmodia quickly multiply in the bloodstream and enter organs, such as the liver and the brain, and start to destroy them.

Symptoms of Malaria

People with malaria suffer from **symptoms** such as fevers, headaches, joint pains, and vomiting. In some cases, they develop brain damage or die. Others seem to get better, but the disease can keep flaring up and causing malarial fevers throughout their lives. There is no cure for malaria.

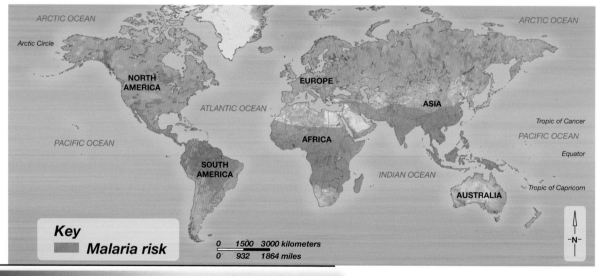

Key
Malaria risk

People are at risk of catching malaria in any of the purple shaded areas.

Did You Know?

Every year about 500 million people are infected with malaria, mostly in tropical regions of the world. Almost one million of these people die from the disease.

Preventing Malaria

If people are bitten by infected mosquitoes, they can take drugs such as quinine, chloroquine, and quinicrine to stop them from getting malaria. However, these drugs are very expensive, and many people cannot afford them. People can also prevent malaria by using insect repellent and mosquito nets to reduce the chance of being bitten. They can drain small pools of water, in which mosquitoes lay their eggs. There is no malaria **vaccine**, although scientists are working hard to find one.

This girl in Senegal, west Africa, is being checked by the doctor as she recovers from malaria.

Bill Gates (1955–)

Bill Gates is a wealthy businessman who founded the Microsoft corporation. Gates and his wife, Melinda, have set up a foundation that works to reduce the number of malaria deaths. They provide money to find a malaria vaccine and determine ways to control mosquitoes.

GLOSSARY WORDS

symptoms   signs that a person may be suffering from a particular disease or illness
vaccine   a small dose of a virus or bacteria injected into patients to help their bodies fight off disease

Measles

Measles is a **contagious** disease caused by a **virus**. It is spread when a person breathes in cough or sneeze droplets from someone who has measles.

Symptoms of Measles

There are many **symptoms** of measles. When people are infected with the virus, they begin to feel tired and unwell. They often develop a fever, a runny nose, a cough, and sore eyes. Patients then develop a rash, which starts on the face and then spreads to the rest of the body. About one-third of people also develop illnesses such as ear infections, **diarrhea**, and pneumonia. If these infections are serious, they might have to go to the hospital.

Measles Vaccine

A measles **vaccine** was developed in the 1960s. Before then, most people caught measles when they were children and then became **immune**, so that they did not get it a second time. Today, in many countries children are given free doses of the Measles-Mumps-Rubella (MMR) vaccine when they are one year old, and again when they are four years old. This vaccine makes them immune to three diseases: measles, mumps, and rubella (also known as German measles).

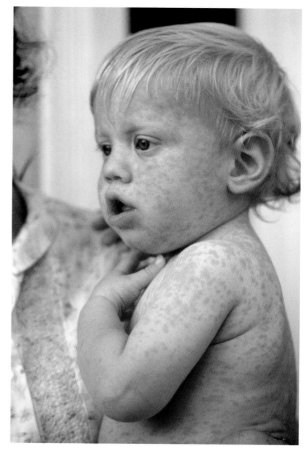

Children with measles develop a red rash all over their bodies.

Did You Know?

There are very few cases of measles in countries such as the United States, where most children are given the MMR vaccine.

German Measles

German measles, or rubella, is caused by a virus that is similar to the measles virus. German measles is generally less severe than measles, and people always recover from it quite quickly. Symptoms include swollen glands, sore joints, and a rash on the face and neck. German measles is dangerous for pregnant women, as it can cause serious problems in unborn babies. Babies who have been exposed to German measles could be born deaf or blind, or could suffer from heart or brain problems.

The rubella virus (magnified here) causes German measles.

Did You Know?

Measles is so contagious that an infected person will probably pass the disease on to about 9 out of every 10 people he or she has contact with, unless those people are already immune.

GLOSSARY WORDS

contagious	passes easily from one person to another
virus	microscopic living particles that stop cells from working properly
symptoms	signs that a person may be suffering from a particular disease or illness
diarrhea	a disorder in the intestines that causes runny feces
vaccine	a small dose of a virus or bacteria injected into patients to help their bodies fight off disease
immune	protected from or resistant to a particular disease

Medicines

Medicines are substances used to cure, treat, or prevent diseases.

Types of Medicines

There are thousands of types of medicines, and some have been used for hundreds of years. In ancient times, most medicines were extracted from plants. Today, some medicines are still made from plants, while others are made in **laboratories**.

Some common types of medicines include:

- analgesics, which treat pain
- antipyretics (say an-tee-pie-RET-iks), which reduce fever
- antibiotics, which kill bacteria
- antihistamines, which treat allergy **symptoms**

Prescription Drugs

Many medicines are drugs that require a doctor's prescription, which is a note from a doctor specifying a particular drug. In order to get these medicines, people need to visit a doctor, who will examine them and decide which medicines they need. The doctor also considers the person's **medical history** before choosing a medicine and writing a prescription. People then take the prescription to the pharmacist, who checks it and gives out the medicine.

Pharmacists give out prescription drugs and explain how to take them correctly.

Did You Know?

Some medicines, such as the painkiller aspirin, can be bought at a supermarket or pharmacy without a prescription.

Herbal Medicines

Herbal medicines are made from herbs and other kinds of plants. Some people use herbal medicines because they believe they are better for the body than pharmacy drugs. Others use herbal medicines along with pharmaceutical medicines. Common herbal medicines include:

- peppermint, which is used to treat digestive problems
- ginger, which is used to treat seasickness
- echinacea, which is used to fight infections

Medicines and Safety

People should never take medicines or drugs that have been prescribed for someone else. They may be allergic, take the wrong dose, or experience dangerous side effects. Medicines should always be stored out of reach of young children. It is important to follow the pharmacist's directions when taking medicines.

Some medicines, such as cough syrup, come in liquid form so that they are easy to swallow.

HEALTH PROFESSIONALS: Pharmacists

Pharmacists are trained to understand how medicines and drugs work. They give out medicine based on a doctor's prescription. They tell people how to use the medicine properly and explain if there are any side effects.

GLOSSARY WORDS

laboratories	rooms in which scientists conduct experiments
symptoms	signs that a person may be suffering from a particular disease or illness
medical history	the history of a patient's illnesses, including what medicines he or she has taken in the past

Mental Health

Mental health is about emotions and feelings of well-being. People suffering from mental health problems may feel sad and unable to cope with stress, work, or friends.

Mental Health Problems

There are many types of mental health problems. Most people feel sad, anxious, cranky, and tired at some times in their lives, particularly during times of stress. For people with mental health problems, these feelings can go on for a long time. They can become so strong that the person loses interest in work and friends, and may stop looking after himself or herself properly. Some people may start to have strange thoughts or **hallucinations**.

Depression

Depression is one of the most common mental health problems. One in five people will suffer from depression at some time in his or her life. People with depression feel very sad for a long time. Depression can be started by a sad event in a person's life or by an ongoing illness. It can also run in families. Some people with depression can be treated with drugs. Some visit a counselor, who can help them talk about and understand the illness.

Some people attend group therapy sessions to talk about mental health problems in a supportive environment.

HEALTH PROFESSIONALS: Psychologists

Psychologists help people talk about issues that may cause depression or other mental health problems. They help patients understand these issues so that they will not cause them as much worry.

Preventing Mental Health Problems

While there is no guaranteed way of preventing mental health problems, there are ways that people can help reduce their chances of developing them. Doctors know that people are less likely to suffer from mental health problems if:

- they have strong networks of friends and family to talk to
- they are members of a group or an organization
- they have a hobby they enjoy

Regular exercise also produces brain chemicals that can help stop some people from developing depression.

During World Mental Health Day, people across the world dress up and march to show their support for people with mental health problems.

Did You Know?

World Mental Health Day is held on October 10 each year. It aims to raise awareness of mental health issues, including how to recognize mental illness and how to get help for sufferers and their loved ones.

GLOSSARY WORD

hallucinations   seeing or hearing things that are not there

Minerals

Minerals are chemical substances that the body needs to stay healthy.

Metabolism

Metabolism (say meh-TAB-uh-LIZ-uhm) is the name for all the chemical reactions that go on in the body to keep a person alive. Some of these reactions require particular minerals. People who eat a balanced **diet** usually get enough minerals from their food.

Potassium and Sodium

Potassium and sodium are minerals that keep the nerves working and the cells healthy. People need about 0.17 ounces (4,700 milligrams) of potassium a day (the weight of about 180 rice grains) and about 0.5 oz (1,500 mg) of sodium a day (the weight of about 60 rice grains). Potassium is found in beans, tomatoes, potato skins, and bananas. Sodium is found in salt, milk, and spinach.

potassium

sodium

These foods all contain either potassium or sodium.

Did You Know?

Zinc is a mineral that is used by many types of cells, including the smell cells in the nose. If people do not have enough zinc, they can lose their sense of smell.

Trace Elements

The body only needs tiny amounts of some minerals. These minerals are called trace elements. Some trace elements are used to make **hormones** or red blood cells. Iron is a trace element that is used to make red blood cells. People need about 0.0002 ounces (8 mg) of iron a day (the weight of about one-third of a rice grain). Iron is found in red meat, leafy green vegetables, eggs, and grains.

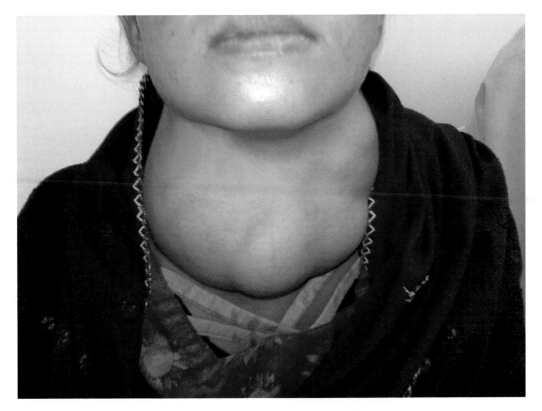

People who lack the trace element iodine may develop a swollen thyroid gland, which is called a goiter (say goy-TER).

George Whipple (1878–1976)

In 1925, American doctor George Whipple discovered that foods containing the mineral iron could cure a disease called pernicious anemia. Before this, the disease killed many people. Whipple and two other researchers were awarded the 1934 Nobel Prize in Medicine for this important work.

GLOSSARY WORDS

diet   the food that a person eats
hormones   chemicals that control how the body works

Multiple Sclerosis

Multiple sclerosis (MS) is a disease that affects the **nervous system**.

Causes of MS

Scientists are not sure what causes MS, but they know that people with MS have faulty nerves. Healthy nerves have a coating around them made of a protein called myelin (say muy-UH-lin). MS causes the body to destroy this myelin coating, leaving scars, or **plaques**, on the nerves. "Sclerosis" means scar and "multiple" indicates that the damage usually occurs in many places.

Symptoms of MS

Symptoms of MS usually develop very gradually, so people often do not realize they are developing the disease. Symptoms can include blurred vision, numbness, weakness, loss of balance, loss of memory, and tiredness. Some people with MS become disabled and cannot look after themselves. Others may experience symptoms once or twice and then have no more symptoms for the rest of their lives.

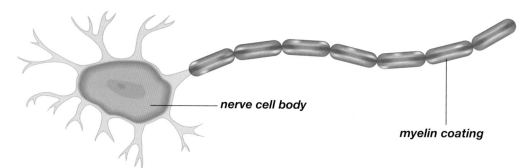

nerve cell body

myelin coating

Jean-Martin Charcot (1825–1893)

French neurologist and professor Jean-Martin Charcot first described the symptoms of MS He named the disease in 1868.

In a healthy nerve, the myelin coating protects the nerve and helps it to function properly.

Cure for MS

There is no cure for MS, but scientists are researching what causes MS and looking for ways to stop it. A group of scientists in New Zealand are trying to put the **gene** that makes human myelin into cows. The cows will then produce milk that contains human myelin. This myelin could be purified and given to people with MS. It is hoped that their bodies would then destroy the myelin from the cows, instead of the natural myelin in the nerves.

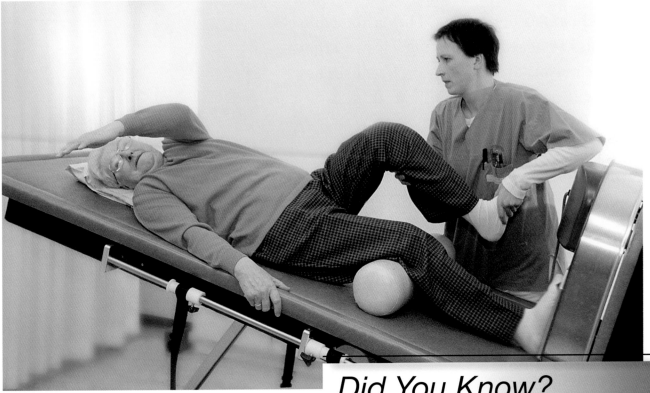

Some people with MS cannot walk because their nerves are extremely scarred, so they need to do regular exercise to keep their muscles healthy.

Did You Know?

More than half a million people around the world have MS. Most people develop the disease between the ages of 20 and 50. It affects twice as many women as men.

GLOSSARY WORDS

nervous system	a system of nerves, cells, and tissues that controls how the body functions
plaques	clumps of dead nerve cells
symptoms	signs that a person may be suffering from a particular disease or illness
gene	part of a chromosome that carries a code for a particular characteristic

Muscles

Muscles contract to move parts of the body.

Types of Muscles

There are three types of muscles in the human body. Skeletal muscles are connected to the skeleton by **tendons**. They are voluntary muscles because a person controls them by thinking about a movement and then doing it. Smooth muscles control the intestines, bladder, stomach, and other organs. The cardiac muscle controls the heart. Smooth muscles and the cardiac muscle are involuntary because they move without a person having to think.

Healthy Muscles

A whole muscle is made of bundles of thousands of muscle fibers. Each muscle fiber is a single cell that is thinner than a human hair. Muscles can change shape depending on how much they are used. When a person exercises a muscle regularly, each of the muscle fibers gradually becomes a little fatter, so that over time the whole muscle gets bigger and more powerful. If a person stops exercising the muscle, it will get smaller again. Exercise also makes the **blood vessels** wider so they can bring more oxygen and food to the muscles, to keep them working longer.

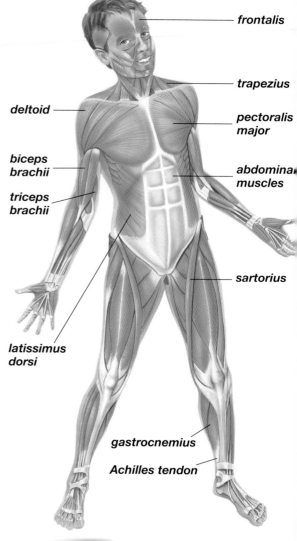

frontalis

trapezius

deltoid

pectoralis major

biceps brachii

abdominal muscles

triceps brachii

sartorius

latissimus dorsi

gastrocnemius

Achilles tendon

HEALTH PROFESSIONALS: Myotherapists

Myotherapists treat muscle pain using massage. Massage loosens tight muscles, helps heal muscle injuries, and relieves headaches and back pain.

There are about 640 skeletal muscles in the human body.

Fast-twitch and Slow-twitch Muscles

Some skeletal muscles are called fast-twitch muscles, while others are called slow-twitch muscles. Fast-twitch muscles are quick and powerful but use large amounts of energy, so they cannot work for long periods. Slow-twitch muscles are less powerful, but they use less energy and so do not tire as easily as fast-twitch muscles.

Muscle Cramps

A muscle cramp is an uncontrollable **spasm** of a muscle. Cramps can last from a few seconds to a few hours, and they generally stop by themselves. Doctors are not sure exactly what causes cramps.

Slow-twitch muscles give marathon runners the stamina to run long distances.

Fast-twitch muscles give weightlifters the strength to lift heavy weights.

Treating Strains

A strain occurs when a person injures his or her tendons or muscles. If a person strains a tendon or muscle, he or she should stop moving, apply an ice pack to the area, and try to raise the muscle above the heart. Sometimes the area may need to be bandaged.

GLOSSARY WORDS

tendons	tough substances that connect bones to muscles
blood vessels	tubes, such as veins or arteries, which blood travels through
spasm	sudden and repeated movements

Nausea

Nausea (say naw-SEE-ah) is a feeling of sickness in the stomach. When people are nauseous, they feel as if they are going to vomit.

Causes of Nausea

Nausea can be caused by infections, **migraines**, strong pain, bad food, and as a side effect from taking medicines. When people are nauseous, they might feel sweaty or dizzy. They start to make more saliva, as if they are about to vomit.

Vomiting

Feeling nauseous often leads to vomiting. Inside a part of the brain called the medulla, there is a vomit center that triggers vomiting. The stomach sends information to the vomit center if a person has eaten too much food or food that is bad. This is the body's way of getting rid of the harmful substance. The blood sends messages to the vomit center if a person takes certain medicines or has an infection. Other parts of the brain send messages to the vomit center when a person sees or thinks about unpleasant sights or smells nasty smells.

Riding on roller coasters can make some people feel nauseous.

Did You Know?

An emetic is a medicine that deliberately causes vomiting. Doctors give emetics if people eat or drink certain types of poisons.

Motion Sickness

Motion sickness is the feeling of nausea people get when they are moving in a particular way. It is sometimes called carsickness, seasickness, or airsickness. Astronauts can even get space sickness.

Motion sickness occurs when the brain becomes confused about whether a person is moving. The brain determines if the body is moving by receiving information from different parts of the body, including the muscles, the eyes, and the liquid in the inner ear. If a person is reading a map while traveling by car along a winding road, the inner ear sends information that the person is moving, while the eyes send information that the person is still. This clash of information in the brain activates the vomit center, causing nausea.

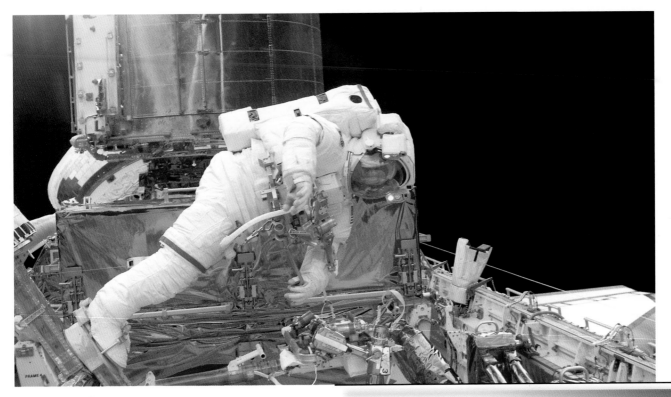

Astronauts sometimes experience nausea in space, and this is called space sickness.

Did You Know?

The idea of nausea is linked to the idea of seasickness. The word "nausea" comes from the Ancient Greek word *naus*, which means "ship."

GLOSSARY WORD

migraines   severe headaches that can last for days

Nerves

Nerves carry tiny electrical messages around the body.

The Nervous System

The nervous system consists of the brain, the spinal cord, and nerves that branch out through the body. Nerves are made of bundles of nerve cells, or neurons. The thickest nerves can be similar to the thickness of a piece of rope, while the thinnest ones are thinner than a human hair. Some nerves carry messages from the **sense organs** to the brain. Other nerves carry messages from the brain to the muscles, to make them move.

Reflex Actions

A reflex action occurs when the body reacts to a sense without thinking about it. Some reflex actions are controlled by the spinal cord so that messages can be processed quickly without involving the brain. Many of the body's reflex actions are quick responses to danger, such as automatically removing the hand from a hot surface or jumping when there is a loud noise.

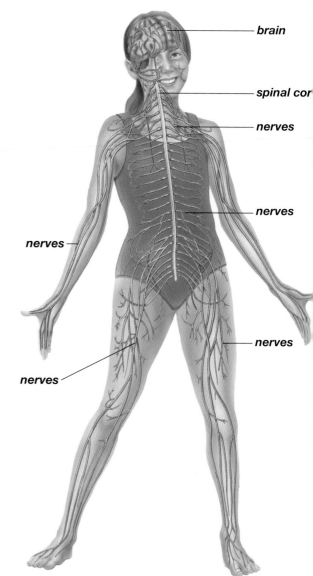

The nervous system is a network of nerves that spread from the spinal cord throughout the body.

Did You Know?

The longest nerve in the human body is the sciatic nerve. It runs from the base of the spinal cord to the feet. If this nerve is damaged or pinched, the pain it causes is called sciatica.

Pinched Nerves

The spinal cord is protected by the bones in the spine, which are called vertebrae (say ver-TUH-bray). Nerves branch off the spinal cord to all parts of the body. Sometimes a nerve can get pinched between the vertebrae, which causes pain and a feeling of "pins and needles." Pinched nerves can also occur in other parts of the body, such as the shoulder.

Paralysis

Paralysis is the loss of movement in parts of the body. If the spinal cord is damaged, then messages traveling to and from the brain are blocked, and unable to reach the muscles.

Paraplegia occurs when the legs and lower part of the body are paralyzed, and it is usually caused by damage lower down the spinal cord. Some people with paraplegia can walk, but most use wheelchairs. Quadriplegia occurs when both arms and legs are paralyzed and is usually caused by damage higher up the spinal cord.

Australian athlete Louise Sauvage is a paraplegic who has won many gold medals at the Paralympic Games.

GLOSSARY WORD

sense organs   organs involved in sensing information from the world, such as the skin, eyes, ears, nose, and tongue

Nose

The nose is the sense organ that allows a person to smell. It is the main airway for the **respiratory system**.

Structure of the Nose

The nose has some parts that can be seen and others that cannot. The visible part of the nose is made of skin, bone, and **cartilage**. Cartilage is flexible, which is why the nose can bend. A wall of cartilage called the septum separates the two nostrils. Behind the visible part of the nose is the nasal cavity. On the top of the nasal cavity is the olfactory epithelium (say ol-FAK-tuh-REE ep-ee-THEE-lee-UHM), which is a patch of nerve cells about the size of a postage stamp. These nerve cells are sensitive to smell molecules.

Smell and Survival

The brain uses smells to tell a person about the environment and keep the person safe. If a person smells burning toast, they immediately recognize the smell and check the toaster. The sense of smell also helps a person choose food and warns of dangerous chemicals.

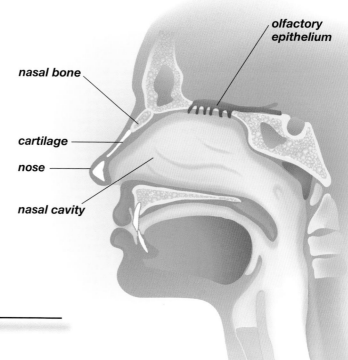

Smell is processed by the olfactory epithelium inside the nasal cavity.

Did You Know?

When someone sneezes, the air and droplets of mucus travel out of the nose at up to 93 miles (150 kilometers) per hour.

Mucus

Mucus protects the nose from bacteria. The inside of the nasal cavity is lined with a wet, thin mucous layer which warms and moistens the air on its way to the lungs. This mucous layer produces mucus, or snot. Mucus contains chemicals that kill bacteria that is breathed into the nose. When people get colds or chest infections, their mucus can turn yellow or green because it contains the white blood cells that have been killed in fighting the infection.

Sneezing

Sneezing is an **involuntary** action that allows the body to remove irritating substances from the nose. The brain, muscles, and nerves in the nose all work together to send dust, pollen, and bacteria flying out of the nose.

Sneezes can be triggered by things such as dust and strong smells.

Did You Know?

The nose also plays a role in taste. In space, astronauts cannot smell easily because smell molecules do not travel into their nasal cavities. Therefore, space food tastes very plain to them.

GLOSSARY WORDS

respiratory system	a system of organs and tubes that controls the body's breathing
cartilage	a strong, flexible substance that cushions bones at the joints
involuntary	uncontrolled

People who are very overweight are said to be obese.

Storing Fat

People become obese when their bodies store large amounts of fat. Food gives people energy and **nutrients** to fuel their bodies. If people eat more food than they need, the excess energy in this food is turned to fat and stored under the skin and around the organs. The organs, including the heart, then have to work harder to keep the body healthy. Obese people also have an increased risk of developing diseases such as **diabetes** and high blood pressure.

Processed Food

Many people become obese because of the types of food they eat. Processed foods such as carbonated drinks, potato chips, and chocolate bars are high in energy, and if this energy is not used, it will be stored as fat.

Eating processed foods can lead to obesity.

Did You Know?

In some developed countries, such as the United States and Australia, obesity is said to be an **epidemic**. It is estimated that more than half the population is overweight in these countries.

Measuring Obesity

Body mass index (BMI) is a calculation used to determine whether someone is overweight or obese. An adult's BMI is calculated by dividing his or her weight in pounds by the square of his or her height in inches, then multiplied by 703. A healthy BMI for most adults is between 20 and 25. Different calculations are used for children, depending on their age.

Preventing Obesity

People can stop themselves from becoming obese by exercising and eating healthy foods. Exercise burns energy, and the more strenuous forms of exercise use the largest amounts of energy. People can perform at least 20 minutes of exercise three or four times a week to help keep their weight healthy and their muscles strong. They can also eat unprocessed foods, such as fruit and vegetables, and drink water instead of sweet drinks to help keep a healthy weight.

It is important for people to exercise regularly to ensure that the food they eat is used up and not turned into fat.

Did You Know?

It takes about half an hour of cycling to burn off the energy in one glass of soft drink.

GLOSSARY WORDS

nutrients	food or chemicals that the body needs to survive
diabetes	a disease in which a person has too much sugar in his or her blood
epidemic	an outbreak of disease that spreads quickly

Index

Page references in bold indicate that there is a full entry for that topic.